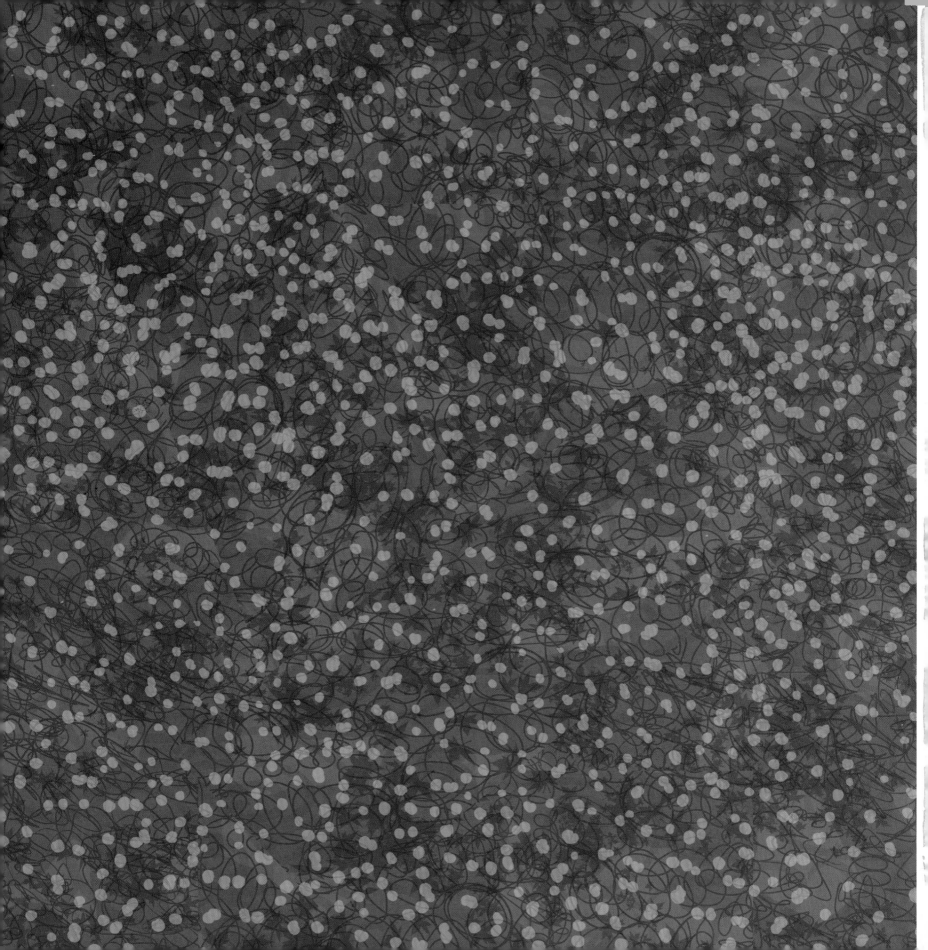

HERE'S WHAT I KNOW SO FAR

Doc's Story

By Diane Till

Designed and Illustrated by Tom Schwartz

With the welcome help of Dr. Tim Roberts, Doc's veterinarian

ACKNOWLEDGEMENTS

To Marie Drake. Brian Manning. Kathe Tanous and Bob Levenson. To Marilyn Taylor, Sue Montgomery, Caroline Powell, Ann Hyman, Joy Lamb, Claudette and Dick Barker and the remarkable women of the First Tuesday Book Club. To Suzi and Godfrey Pflager. Friend and editor, Anne Gillis. My deepest thanks to you all. And to Jane Talcott, what can I say? You introduced me to the brilliantly talented Tom Schwartz, and he brought Doc to life.

Diane Till

HERE'S WHAT I KNOW SO FAR
Doc's Story

Requests for permission to make copies of any part of the work should be mailed to: Permissions Department, Ocean Publishing, P.O. Box 1080, Flagler Beach, FL 32136.

Text copyright © 2007 by Diane Till
Cover, jacket and illustrations copyright © 2007 by Tom Schwartz

Library of Congress Control Number 2007922693

ISBN-13 978-0-9767291-7-4

Printed and bound in the United States of America

Ocean Publishing
P.O. Box 1080
Flagler Beach, FL 32136
www.ocean-publishing.com

Welcome. This may be a bit different from other children's books you've read. For example, I encourage you to start at the beginning, the middle or the end. Feel free to read it front to back or back to front. Read just a page or two a day. Read only Doc's point of view, and leave Dr. Tim's comments for later. Or read them both together. But whenever you pick up Doc's story, I hope you will take your time, and get to know Doc and how he learns about his world.

I have always been so grateful for the friendship of my dogs. But they can certainly be a mystery. My dog Jack is never so happy as when he finds a dead fish down by the river. He celebrates his find by lying on his back and rolling all over it. My dog Gypsy was a sociable city dog and was never more miserable than during one summer we spent in the country where there were no other dogs. My dog Emma had a great sense of humor and would invent games. My least favorite was when she would run in circles around me just out of my reach, and I swear she was laughing at me the whole time.

Now I know there are many opinions on dog behavior and training. This book is my attempt to get into the mind of a dog and let us learn from his take on his life and the strange humans he lives with and tries to please. Dr. Tim Roberts comes along to explain what the dog is going through and how to teach good behavior — in the dog and in us. I hope that Doc can maybe help us all be a bit more understanding. I hope kids will learn why a good parent sometimes has to say "no." And I hope parents will learn the great importance of play. Above all else, I hope anyone who picks up this book will have some fun.

Diane Till

HERE'S WHAT I KNOW SO FAR.

It's dark. I can't see.
There seem to be others here just like me.
We line up to eat, fall asleep in a heap.
Someone said, "Daddy, can I have one to keep?
Oh, look at that one. He's so sweet."
My eyes flew open and I saw Polly's feet.

Well, what's the first thing *your* eyes ever saw?
Was it your mother's face? Or maybe her paw?
Not me. Two little feet with bright pink toes
attached to a girl in bright pink clothes.
Then two little hands swooped me up in a hug.
She nuzzled my face, gave my ears a tug.
I quite liked this. So, I gave her a kiss.

AND THAT'S WHAT I KNOW SO FAR.

Dr. Tim's Message: When puppies are born, their eyes are shut tight. Then, when they're about ten days old, they open their eyes and see their brand new world. The first few weeks puppies just eat, sleep and cuddle close to their mother. New puppies can have as many as four or five, or eight or nine brothers and sisters. Or even more!

All puppies need a lot of sleep. Don't play with them too much for the first few days. It's OK to pat them, but be very gentle. Once their eyes open, they become more curious and playful every day. Just like you.

HERE'S WHAT I KNOW SO FAR.

I'm eight weeks old, and life is so exciting.
All day we play or pretend to be fighting,
my three sisters, my brother and me.
I climbed out of our box to go explore,
and almost made it to the kitchen door.

They put me back in my box, close to my mother.
I scrambled up her side and then fell on my brother.
Mom nuzzled us softly with her nose.
We scooted under her chin and curled up close,
where it's quiet and comfy, a nice place to doze.

AND THAT'S WHAT I KNOW SO FAR.

Dr. Tim's Message: Of course, you want to bring your new puppy home right away, but be patient. It's best if he stays with his mother for at least 8 weeks. Time with mom and his littermates is important. It helps create confidence in the puppy, that in turn helps him become a secure adult dog.

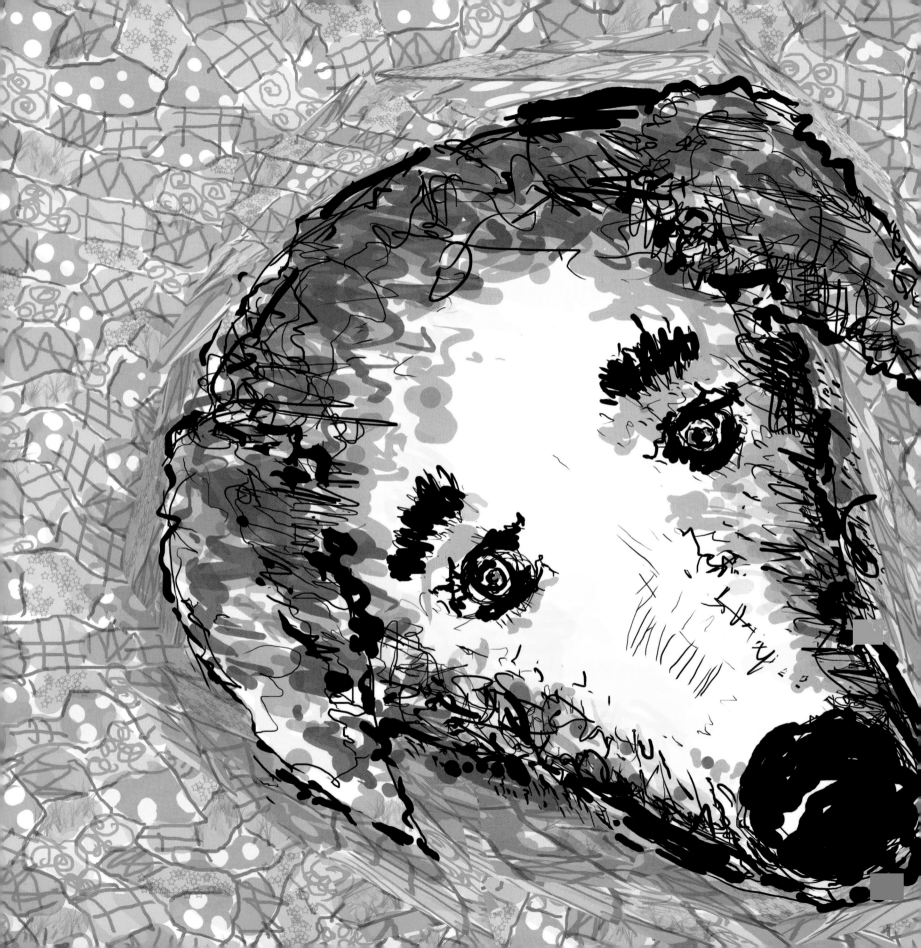

HERE'S WHAT I KNOW SO FAR.

The little girl named Polly came back again today.
She wrapped me in a quilt and took me away.

Dr. Tim's Message: Big day. The puppy is coming home, and you need to be ready. He'll need his own place. A large box or a small warm room will do, but a dog crate is best. Don't worry. You're not locking him in a cage. You're giving him his own home. Even grownup dogs wander back to their crates to lie down.

Give your puppy a couple of comfortable, washable blankets or towels to curl up in. Also some chew toys. If you've arranged a box instead of a crate, put the box in the bathroom and close the door overnight. Be sure puppy food and a water dish are nearby.

What the puppy needs most is love, but be gentle. There'll be plenty of time for roughhousing later. Try to make the first few days a quiet time, so the puppy can gradually get adjusted to you and his new family.

Remember this little guy is going to be your very best friend. Now's the time to start building trust and love.

HERE'S WHAT I KNOW SO FAR.

I'm in my crate with just a blanket and a bone.
I'm scared. It's late and I'm all alone.
I want my mom.
I want my mom!
I'll try not to cry,
But why oh why
am I here all alone?
Yip-yip. Yip! Yipe! Yipe-yipe-yipe-yipe! Yipe!
Wait. There's a light down the hall.
Polly's coming after all.
She whispers, "Don't worry, Puppy, I'm here."
Maybe I'll sleep now. There's nothing to fear.

AND THAT'S WHAT I (YAWN) KNOW SO FAR.

Dr. Tim's Message: Poor little pup. It's scary being away from his mother in a strange new place. He'll probably cry when he wakes up during the first few nights until he learns that he's truly safe.

Before you go to bed take him out for a last bathroom visit. Then leave him in his crate with his toys and a soft towel or blanket.

The crate is a good way to start the housebreaking process because puppies don't like to pee where they sleep. When you take your puppy out, always take him to the same spot. The smell will be familiar, which reminds him what he's supposed to do. Even though you're tired and it's late, praise him when he succeeds.

After a couple of weeks your puppy will be able to make it through the night. But take him outside first thing in the morning, so he can start to get the idea that his "bathroom" is outside.

What I *am* seems to be the mystery.
Polly's dad claims I have quite a history.
Polly's mom says I'm part retriever.
But don't you believe her.
I won't fetch. And I don't catch.
The question is what breed do I match?

I'm not a shepherd or a hound.
I'm not some toy, all fuzzy and round.
I'm not a poodle, so pampered and hyper.
Or an over-bred spaniel in need of a diaper.
I don't think I'm a terrier because I'm not yappy.
But whatever I am, I'm certainly happy.

My family tree has a unique pedigree.
It produced this brilliant, one-of-a-kind Me!

AND THAT'S WHAT I KNOW SO FAR.

Dr. Tim's Message: Did you know that all dogs are descended from the wolf? Thousands of years ago people probably tamed and raised some wolf puppies. It was a smart thing to do. Wolves, like us, live in families and they learn that it's their job to protect the family.

Dogs do so much for us. They've been taught to hunt. To retrieve birds. To go into tunnels after rats and moles. To herd sheep and cattle. To protect the farm. To track down criminals. To sniff and detect drugs. To help the blind, the elderly and the handicapped. To search for and rescue people lost in an avalanche or an earthquake. And of course, to be members of the family.

Today the American Kennel Club (AKC) recognizes over 150 breeds of dog. Great Danes to Chihuahuas. Cocker Spaniels and Collies. German Shepherds, French Poodles, English Sheepdogs, Hungarian Pulik, Portuguese Water Dogs, Irish Wolfhounds, Chinese Shar-peis - there's a whole world of breeds, and each has special abilities to help mankind.

But without a doubt, the most valuable gift our dogs give us is their absolute unconditional love.

HERE'S WHAT I KNOW SO FAR.

It's been like a puzzle. It's been like a game.
The family had trouble choosing my name.
So, I never knew what to answer to.
First, I was Fritz, then I was Mack.
Then they tried Barney, Amos, and Jack.
For a while I was Jiggs, then Piddles, and Sam.
And for one horrible week, they called me Kazaam!

But, it seems there's something about my face.
They'd look at me closely, day after day.
"What's your name, little dog?
What's your face trying to say?"

Polly said, "There *is* something about his face.
He looks like a doctor. His face seems to say,
'How do you feel? Are you *sure* you're OK?'"
So, Polly named me Doc, and it's Doc I'll stay.

AND THAT'S WHAT I KNOW SO FAR.

Piddles

DOC!!

MACK

Jiggs

Barney

KAZAAM

JACK

Dr. Tim's Message: It's funny how puppies almost do seem to *tell us* what to name them. Dogs have distinct personalities. Some are sweet and cuddly. Some are balls of energy. Some are proud and alert. And some are goofy as circus clowns.

A true fun-loving, adventure-seeking, confident dog deserves a very good name. Watch your puppy and play with him for a few days. You'll see. All of a sudden, you'll just *know* his name.

Why walk when you can run?
Walking on a leash is just no fun.

I can sniff the news. It's in the air.
I'll follow my nose most anywhere.
I'll track a scent to see where it goes.
And even running, I never stub my nose.

Sniff-sniff. Holly the Collie came to *my* yard to pee!
Sniff-sniff. Maggie, the Springer, was here by this tree.
Oh please, Polly, please. Stop *pulling* on me.
OK. I'll show you! Instead of walking, I'll run.
I'll run in circles, round and round.
Oops. I just toppled Polly to the ground.

AND THAT'S WHAT I KNOW SO FAR.

Dr. Tim's Message: Puppies want to run, to sniff and explore. But they need to learn to walk on a leash. Carry some treats so pup learns that good behavior has rewards. Hold the leash just tight enough so your dog is under your control, being careful not to choke him. Say, "Walk," and start walking. If your puppy tries to run ahead, firmly repeat the word, "Walk." At the same time, give a quick light pull to the leash, to bring him back to your side. When he succeeds, give him a treat and praise.

A keyed up dog is impossible to train (just like a keyed up kid). So be sure to include lots of free-run playtime.

Dogs are extremely sensitive to your tone of voice. You can say, "You are the world's best dog." But if you're yelling it in an angry tone, your pup will tremble in fear. Puppies know an "I mean business" tone of voice when they hear it. Well, you do too, don't you?

HERE'S WHAT I KNOW SO FAR.

Life has wonderful things to do.
But the absolute best is to chew.
Listen. I'll chew whatever's there:
The corner of a rug, the leg of a chair.
I love to chew on a shoe.
Sneakers, sandals, loafers. Any shoe will do.
I love to chew a pillow and *grrrrr-rip* it to shreds,
until feathers swirl around my head.
And if ever I find that I am bored?
Well, I can simply chew an electric cord.

Polly's mom said, "That's it. No more!
C'mon we're off to that new pet store."
So, now there's a basket of chew toys galore.
But Polly and I know what old socks are for:
Games of rollicking, rousing tug-o-war!

AND THAT'S WHAT I KNOW SO FAR.

Dr. Tim's Message: Puppies have very sharp little teeth. They lose their baby teeth at about six months. Chewing things helps during teething. But puppies, and dogs for that matter, *need* to chew. It's a natural part of dog behavior.

Be sure to have chew toys on hand. If puppies don't have a toy, they'll find something else. And aside from the damage they can cause, many things around the house are dangerous. Some houseplants are poisonous. An electric cord could give a puppy a shock. And shoes, rugs, pillows and chairs are expensive for your parents to replace.

Lonely and bored dogs are sad, not bad, but they will get into trouble. They are used to their rough-and-tumble life with their brothers and sisters. In a new home, they'll look for things to do.

So, take your puppy for walks, play tug of war, invent a game. Some dogs are even great at hide & seek. Just remember, your puppy's absolute favorite "toy" is you. So yes, spend time training him to walk, sit and stay. But never *ever* forget to play.

You won't *believe* the places
where you're not supposed to pee.
They go crazy if you pee on a chair.
"No, Doc, nooooo. Don't pee there."
And heaven help you if you're up on the bed.
Pee on a bed and you'll wish you were dead.

You can't pee in the kitchen or in the hall.
On the carpet? Oh man, don't pee there at all.
Actually, you shouldn't pee on any floor.
If you need to go, give a scratch at the door.
They'll let you out. You'll know what to do.
And they say "Good boy" when you're through.

AND THAT'S WHAT I KNOW SO FAR.

Dr. Tim's Message: Housetraining a puppy is a lot like training you. It takes consistency. And kindness. "No" doesn't mean "maybe." And shouting doesn't help.

Puppies need to go out 8 to 10 times a day: after they eat or drink, first thing in the morning and last thing at night. Take your pup out anytime he wakes up or after he's been playing hard. Puppies have small bladders. They want to please you, but they can't wait too long.

Watch your pup carefully. If he scurries out of your sight, it may be to pee. If you catch him just starting to pee, clap your hands hard or make a sharp noise. This will startle him. Catch him in mid-pee, scoop up the pup and take him outside.

Never rub his nose in it or swat him with a newspaper. He's a puppy. He won't understand, and you'll just create more problems.

Puppies get excited easily. When you come home, your puppy will react as if you've been gone for days, which may also result in an excited dribble or two. Try to put him outside immediately. And don't worry. He will soon become a well-mannered housebroken dog.

BARK

HOWL

SCRATC

cha

HERE'S WHAT I KNOW SO FAR.

Have you been to see a vet yet?

How many shots did *you* have to get?

Dr. Tim checked my eyes. He inspected each ear.

He felt my tummy. He examined my rear.

I was so insulted,

it nearly resulted

with me biting his hand.

But he gave me a scratch, a treat and a pat.

He said, "Good boy." And that was that.

cock·a·doodle·do

MEOW

SPIT

YAP SHOUT JUMP

SCREAM

The waiting room made up for it all.
It was a howling, screaming, barking ball.
Not my fault. Well, not precisely.
We were all sitting there, waiting nicely,
two Yorkies, a basset, a parrot and me.
A man walked in with an obnoxious cat.
I barked (wouldn't you?). The cat spat,
scratched the man, and jumped free.
The Yorkies were yapping, the basset was baying.
Well, of course, I thought we were playing.
So I got loose and chased the cat.
My leash tripped the man who went down *splat*.
Everyone was shouting or barking, a quite rowdy crew.
Until the parrot screamed "Cocka-doodle-do."
He was copying a rooster he'd heard on TV.
Then everybody laughed. Even me.

AND THAT'S WHAT I KNOW SO FAR.

Dr. Tim's Message: You get vaccinations, and so does your puppy. He gets his first shot when he's six weeks old, followed by three booster shots. Then when he's sixteen weeks old, he gets his first rabies shot.
Dogs get rabies shots every year, which is a good time for an overall checkup. For obvious reasons, please make sure your dog is on a leash and your cat is in a pet carrier when you visit the veterinarian.

HERE'S WHAT I KNOW SO FAR (FUNNY THINGS).

Polly's aunt said I tickle her funny bone.
Don't think I've ever *chewed* on a funny bone.
Is it like a hambone? Or maybe a rib?
If you have one handy, I'll tie on my bib.

Shhhh. Did you see it? It's trying to find me.
Look! There. It's sneaking up behind me.
I'll catch it, snatch it and throw it to the ground.
Now we're racing in circles, round and round.
I've almost got it. I won't fail!
Hey wait a minute. I'm chasing my tail.

I'm fast asleep, curled up with my toys.
I start to make a yelping noise.
My eyelids flutter. My tail thumps the floor.
My feet twitch. And I start to snore.
Know what I'm doing? It is what it seems.
I'm lying here having wonderful dreams.

Uh-oh. What's this? I keep going 'Hic!'
What does it - Hic! - mean? Am I sick?
Why is Polly laughing at me? Hic!
Am I performing some sort of trick?
Hic?

AND THAT'S WHAT I KNOW SO FAR.

Dr. Tim's Message: It's not possible to watch a puppy chase his tail without laughing. Puppies do get hiccups, and when they do, they look so surprised. But it's nothing to worry about. They grow out of it. Dogs do dream, although little is known about what they dream. Chasing a rabbit? Catching a ball? Or, maybe it's a dream about playing with you.

HERE'S WHAT I KNOW SO FAR.

Don't you just hate the word 'No?'
I do. I hate the word 'No.'
You invent a game and dig up some flowers.
And what do you get? "No, Doc. No!"
You roll in the mud and play in the showers.
And again, they say, "No, Doc. No!"

One day the garbage had a really great smell.
I tore through the bag because I could tell
it contained what remained of a big broiled fish.
I rolled all over it. The fish went squish.
My coat was greasy, my smell stupendous!
Polly said, "*Eeeeuuu*, your smell's horrendous.
I wagged my tail to make her laugh.
But she put me in a tub and gave me a bath,
saying the whole time, *"No, Doc, No!"*

AND THAT'S WHAT I KNOW SO FAR.

Dr. Tim's Message: Dogs do roll in truly awful things. Here is a best guess reason why. Dogs are descended from wolves. Wolves live in the wild and want very much to avoid being the dinner of a mountain lion. Animals hunt by smell. So if a wolf found something foul to roll in, the smell would serve to disguise his real identity. So, perhaps disguising itself with smell is an instinct developed thousands of years ago when your fluffy puppy was a wolf.

Or, for all we know, maybe it's just fun.

I like the FedEx guy and the guy from UPS.
And Mr. Barstow, the mailman, he's OK, I guess.
But if I smell a stranger coming to do us harm,
I'll snarl, bark and growl and raise the alarm.

My friend Holly the Collie almost died today.
You know, the one who comes to my house to play?
Well, her family left her locked in their car.
They weren't gone long. They didn't go far.
But she had a stroke. The heat was to blame.
Dr. Tim sighed, "She'll never be the same."

Why do humans cry?
Why do tears taste like salt?
What makes humans sad?
Is it somehow my fault?

AND THAT'S WHAT I KNOW SO FAR.

Dr. Tim's Message: A dog's hearing is at least twice as sharp as ours. And their sense of smell is easily a million times better than ours! So they are well equipped to let us know if strangers are approaching the house. Your dog will protect any area he considers part of his territory and all members of his family. And, when it comes to family, you are number one!

If you walk into another dog's territory, be careful. Watch the dog. He may raise his hackles, which means the fur on his neck and down the top of his back will stand on end. This is usually a sign that he's alert to possible attack. If he is standing stiff-legged with head a bit lowered, eyes looking right at you, back slowly away.

Never, never leave your dog in a car. Even if you're just running into the store for five minutes. That's all it can take. When humans are hot, we sweat. Dogs can't sweat. They just open their mouths and pant. Panting dehydrates the dog, and unless he gets relief, he will soon suffer a heat stroke and die.

HERE'S WHAT I KNOW SO FAR.
I think I'm smart. I know I'm brave.
Well, occasionally I misbehave.
Sure, I jump up on people. I think it's cool.
But, the family took me off to Obedience School.

My trainer was so impressed she gave me an "A."
And now I know how to come, I know how to stay.
I know where to pee. And what not to chew.
I don't pull on the leash. Except when I do.
Behaving *all* the time is such a chore.
I try my best, but what a bore.
I've thought it over and here's what I say:
If I had my way, we'd just play all day!

AND THAT'S WHAT I KNOW SO FAR.

Dr. Tim's Message: It's true. One day, your dog just seems to get it. You'll say, "Come" in a proper I-mean-business voice. Your dog will look at you to see if you really mean it. You can almost see what's going on in his puppy brain: "Hmmm, do I dare run away? Or should I obey?" And then miracle of miracles, he trots over to you and sits quietly by your side.

You are on the way to a well-behaved, well-adjusted happy dog. But be consistent. A dog won't remember he's not supposed to jump on people if it's sometimes encouraged.

Another word about consistency: Always be consistent with your praise. Your dog wants nothing more than to please you. Praise when he does is a much more effective training method than shouting when he doesn't.

HERE'S WHAT I KNOW SO FAR.

I wait for Polly to come home from school.
Fun before homework. That's our rule.
I'm her audience when she plays guitar.
I'm her biggest fan. She's the star.

I'm seven in human years, one in mine.
To celebrate my birthday we had a great time.
Polly and the family gave me a "cake."
They put a candle in a piece of steak.

I made a wish, and I hope it comes true.
I wish that one day soon, I could meet you.

AND THAT'S WHAT I KNOW SO FAR.